D0236253

JAGUAR
The Legend

JAGUAR
The Legend

Jonathan Wood

Page 1: The Jaguar mascot, the work of The Autocar's *famous artist, Frederick Gordon Crosby, graced the company's cars between 1937 and 1968. Page 2: A 1958 American-registered XK 150S roadster, with an XK 120 in the background. The US, then as now, is Jaguar's principal overseas market. Page 3: The scarce XKSS of 1957 was a roadgoing version of the Le Mans-winning D-Type. Below right: Jaguar's founder, William Lyons, began his remarkable career by creating the Austin Swallow Seven and this is its Swallow mascot.*

Figures and data in this book are quoted in metric measurements first, with the Imperial equivalents noted in brackets.

This is a Parragon Book

© Parragon 1997
Reprinted in 1998

Parragon Publishing
13 Whiteladies Road
Clifton
Bristol BS8 1PB

Designed, produced and packaged by
Touchstone
Old Chapel Studio, Plain Road, Marden,
Tonbridge, Kent TN12 9LS, United Kingdom

Edited by Philip de Ste. Croix

ISBN 0-75252-069-5

Printed in Italy

Photographic credits:

All photographs by **Neill Bruce Motoring Photolibrary**, with the exception of the following:
(Abbreviations: r=right, l=left, t=top, b=below)

Peter Roberts Collection c/o Neill Bruce: 6-7, 61 (*br*), 64, 65(*t*), 74.

Peter Roberts © Neill Bruce: 5, 11(*b*), 15(*t*).

Paul Skilleter: 11(*t*), 58-59.

Bay View Books Ltd: 40-41.

Jaguar Daimler Heritage Trust: 62-63, 66.

Jaguar Cars Ltd: 75-79.

Neill Bruce and the publishers would like to thank the many owners who have made their cars available for photography, including the following:

Jaguar Cars Ltd: XJ220s and XJ13.

Nigel Dawes: S.S.90; S.S.100; Mk V; XK 120 coupé and drophead; Shortnose D-Type; XKSS; 3.8 Mk II; 4.2 S1 E-Type; the ex-Bardinon & Briggs Cunningham Lightweight E-Types.

Terry Cohn: XK 120 roadster and XK 150 roadster.

Brooks Auctioneers: Mk VII; XK 140; XK 150 drophead; 3.8 S1 E-Type; Mk X, XJ6 series 1 and SIII E-Types.

Mike Barker at **The Midland Motor Museum:** XK150 coupé and XJR-S Celebration coupé.

Duncan Hamilton Ltd: Le Mans C-Type.

The Haynes Sparkford Motor Museum: XJS convertible.

The Earl of March for the wonderful Goodwood Festival of Speed.

Contents

Introduction

JAGUAR! For over 50 years this name has been identified with the best of British automobile engineering as a make that offers its customers stylish, refined high performance cars at a price that they can afford.

Like many of the great names of motoring history, Jaguar was the creation one man. He was Blackpool born William Lyons (1901-1985), a stylist of the highest order, whose talent created the indefinable and memorable 'Jaguar look'.

The marque's origins are to be found in Lyons' native Blackpool, where in 1922 he and a partner

began to manufacture motorcycle sidecars that they marketed under the Swallow name. Later the firm diversified into coachbuilding and in 1927 produced its first car, a curvaceous, open, two-seater sports, Austin Seven-based model called the Austin Swallow. A move to Coventry, at the very heart of the British motor industry, followed at the end of 1928.

Left: Sir William Lyons, one of the British motor industry's outstanding personalities and creator of the S.S. and Jaguar marques. Above: Swallow Model 4 motorcycle sidecars under construction that began in Blackpool and is here continuing at Foleshill, Coventry. Production continued there until 1944.

Later, in 1931 and in the teeth of the world depression, Lyons launched the stunning, value for money S.S. car, predecessor of the Jaguar. This was a difficult time for any motor manufacturer but Lyons had proved himself to be financially shrewd and was a fine judge of engineering talent.

In these pre-war days, S.S. had to rely on Standard-based engines but in 1935 William Heynes joined the company and he was later to become its respected chief engineer. The team of which he was the first member went on to create the legendary high performance, twin-overhead-camshaft XK engine that appeared in 1948 and would go on to power every Jaguar built between 1950 and 1971.

Its creation was a high risk strategy for such a relatively small company but Lyons' team had created one of the world's great engines. Its success was at the heart of Jaguar's post-war growth and this robust six enjoyed a 44-year manufacturing run: production did not cease until 1992.

In 1945 Jaguar, hitherto a model name, had replaced that of S.S. with its Nazi taint. In an expansive post-war world the XK engine first appeared under the bonnet of Jaguar's famous XK120 sports car but it had been designed for a 160km/h (100mph) saloon that appeared as the commodious Mark VII in 1950.

However, the unit's advanced specification also led to the creation of the company's sports

Below: Stirling Moss at the wheel of the 1957 XKSS 704 in the early 1970s. He appeared in a film to commemorate the Sebring 12-hour race won by a D-Type Jaguar in 1955.

Above: The Mark VII saloon of 1951/54, for which Jaguar's famous XK six-cylinder, twin-overhead-camshaft engine was developed. This model found favour in America.

racing C and D-types that provided Jaguar with no less than five celebrated victories at the Le Mans 24 hour race during the 1950s.

These triumphs ensured that the Jaguar name became world famous and provided the publicity that Sir William, as he became in 1956, required to sell his sleek, powerful and increasingly impressive saloons.

For although the marque is forever identified with sports cars, the reality is that the company has, from the very outset, primarily been a manufacturer of closed cars, with the memorable but low production and less profitable sports models always playing second fiddle to them in the affections of its enigmatic founder.

Today the Lyons legacy is in the safe hands of the Ford Motor Company as owners of a revitalized Jaguar, as it prepares to meet the challenges and demands of the 21st century.

7

Austin Swallow Seven

THE SWALLOW Sidecar Company began life in a modest way at Blackpool in 1922, the same year in which Austin launched its famous Seven. Specialist coachbuilders were soon offering their own bodies on its diminutive but robust chassis and William Lyons decided to follow suit.

The outcome was a rounded and stylish open two-seater touring body with its own distinctive radiator shell, although no changes were made to the chassis or engine.

Announced in May 1927, the Austin Swallow Seven, at £175, was £30 more expensive than the no-frills, but four-seater, Austin version. A detachable hardtop was £10 extra.

The model was well received. Customers would order chassis from their local agents, whereupon they were dispatched to Blackpool by train. But Lyons soon found that his cramped premises, at Cocker Street, was unable to cope with demand. Chassis were building up in the yard at nearby Talbot Street Station and the stationmaster was 'raising hell'.

In the meantime Swallow had created a saloon version of the design, which appeared in mid-1928. This was even more striking than the tourer with colourful two-tone paintwork brought to a 'pin nib' point at the radiator. Earlier Lyons had taken an example to London distributor Bert Henly, who promptly ordered 500!

The trouble was that no more than 14 cars could be produced at Blackpool each week. There was only one thing for it. Swallow needed larger premises and Lyons took the opportunity of moving his small company to Coventry, which was the hub of the British motor industry. There he found what he was looking for at a former shell filling factory at Holbrook Lane in the Foleshill district of the city.

The move was effected between October and November of 1928 and production soon restarted. In addition to the Austin Swallow Seven, Lyons began bodying Fiat, Standard, Swift and Wolseley chassis which meant that output rose to around the 100-a-week mark.

However, none of these versions matched the success of the original Austin Swallow. By the time that production ceased in the summer of 1932, some 3500 examples of the tourer and saloon had been built. But by then Lyons was fully occupied with his own car, the S.S.1, which had been launched in the previous year.

Left and right: An Austin Swallow Seven of 1931 vintage that displayed Lyons' flair for innovative coachwork. Produced both in Blackpool and Coventry, this example features the fifth and final version of the distinctive radiator cowl. The model was also produced in touring form.

SPECIFICATION	AUSTIN SWALLOW SEVEN
ENGINE	Straight 4, 747cc
HORSEPOWER	10.5hp @ 2400rpm
TRANSMISSION	Manual 3-speed
CHASSIS	Channel section A-frame
SUSPENSION	Transverse leaf front, quarter elliptic rear
BRAKES	Cable-operated drum
TOP SPEED	80km/h (50mph)
ACCELERATION	0-60km/h (40mph): 37 seconds

Right: The Swallow's leather-trimmed interior was much more luxurious than the Austin version. The nearside glove compartment included a Ladies Companion set.

9

S.S.1

SPECIFICATION	S.S.1 (16hp)
ENGINE	Straight 6, 2054cc
HORSEPOWER	45bhp @ 3800rpm
TRANSMISSION	Manual 4-speed
CHASSIS	Channel section
SUSPENSION	Leaf spring front and rear
BRAKES	Bendix cable operated
TOP SPEED	113km/h (70mph)
ACCELERATION	0-80km/h (50mph): 20 seconds

THE JAGUAR story really begins with this car, the S.S.1, the first of the S.S. line. The success, in particular, of the Austin Swallow convinced William Lyons of the commercial potential of his special brand of coachwork.

But his designs were constrained by the use of a manufacturer's existing chassis. He therefore had a purpose-designed frame made for him by Rubery Owen that could accommodate the engines and running gear of Standard's 16 and 20hp models.

These applications were the outcome of a dialogue between Lyons and the Coventry company's chairman, Reginald Maudslay, and general manager John Black. It centred on the use of Standard components and also about what Lyons' car was to be called.

The S.S. name was decided upon but, as Lyons later recalled, 'whether it stood for Standard Swallow or Swallow Special . . . was never resolved.'

The first car, powered by Standard's 16hp, 2 litre, side-valve, six-cylinder engine, was displayed at the 1931 Motor Show which, as usual, was held in October.

This unmodified unit played host to an adventurous coupé body with a long bonnet ahead of low browed, fixed-head coachwork, distinguished by the use of imitation pram-type handles. Cycle-type front wings were employed as there were no running boards.

The overall impression was of a low, stylish and supremely elegant creation in the best Continental traditions, whilst the S.S.1's price was equally sensational. The *Daily Express* heralded the coupé as 'The car with the £1000 look for £300.' The actual figure was £312 and an extra £10 would secure the 2.5 litre, 20hp engine. Performance was less impressive although the S.S.1 could be coaxed to 112km/h (70mph).

The model was radically revised for the 1933 season with a new chassis that allowed the rear axle to sit above the chassis members whilst the bodywork was also altered. This now featured more conventional wings and running boards, and the coupé was joined by a four-seater tourer.

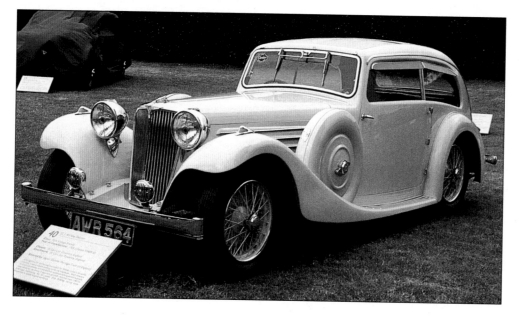

Left: A 1935 S.S.1 coupé. It was not one of Lyons' favourite designs! Above right: The S.S.1 coupé, one of 502 built. The pram handles did not fold. Right: An S.S.1 four-seater tourer of 1933, the first year of production. All of these cars used Standard 16 and 20hp engines.

In the following year came the first S.S. saloon, a conventional and elegant two-door design, which was joined for 1935 by the pillarless Airline that featured fashionable ideas about streamlining. Since 1934 the S.S.1's had benefited from Standard having enlarged its engines to 2.1 and 2.6 litres.

The model remained in production until 1936, a respectable 4254 examples having been built. Meanwhile William Lyons had been discovering how to make his cars go faster . . .

S.S.90

JAGUAR sports cars have consistently been distinguished by their elegant, finely proportioned bodywork. It is a tradition that can be traced back to the S.S.90 which was William Lyons' first sports car.

Ironically, such models were always of secondary commercial importance to Lyons. It was therefore three and a half years after the S.S.1 had made its debut that the company introduced the 90 in March 1935.

It was so called because it was capable of a respectable 144km/h (90mph) and was based on a shortened version of the S.S.1 chassis, in which 381mm (15in) had been removed from the centre section.

Unlike the mainstream models, there was no choice of engine. The 90 was only available with Standard's 2.6 litre, 20hp side valver although some ministrations were made to the unit. The 1935 S.S. range had benefited from a compression ratio raised from 6 to 7:1 and twin RAG carburettors. In addition, the 90's engine had a balanced crankshaft and high-lift camshaft.

The customary half-elliptic springs were augmented by the provision of Telecontrol and Hartford shock absorbers.

But, as ever, it was the coachwork that proclaimed the sophistication of the S.S. approach.

Lyons' first sports car, the 90, appeared in 1935 and this Standard side-valve-engined model was only built in that year. It subsequently evolved into the more potent S.S.100.

The long bonnet and flowing wings found echoes in the 1934 S.S.1 range but the 90 was an open two-seater in its own right, although only the prototype featured a graceful rounded tail. The remaining cars used a more conventional slab-type petrol tank and vertical spare wheel. Typically, the price was a competitive £395.

The reality was that the 90 was destined for a relatively brief manufacturing life, the last car being built in November 1935. Only 23 examples were made.

One 90 was run in the 1935 RAC Rally, held in the model's introductory month, driven by the Hon. Brian Lewis. Unfortunately its clutch failed, although he put up a spectacular performance in the subsequent eliminating trials.

Yet time was running out for the side-valve-engined S.S.s. William Heynes had arrived at the Foleshill factory as chief engineer in 1935 to see the first of the overhead-valve S.S. Jaguars into production for the 1936 season.

This transformed the 90 into one of Lyons' most famous sports cars, the 160km/h (100mph) S.S.100, that was built until the outbreak of war.

Right: The 90's handsome dashboard with speedometer reading to 100mph (161km/h). The steering wheel, with ignition and lighting controls in the middle, was non-adjustable so the car was driven 'elbows out'. Below: The underslung chassis at the rear contributed to the model's low look that survived, in essence, until 1939. Like its many open two-seater contemporaries, the 90's body was coachbuilt and made of aluminium, hand-beaten on an ash frame.

SPECIFICATION	S.S.90
ENGINE	Straight 6, 2663cc
HORSEPOWER	70bhp @ 4000rpm
TRANSMISSION	Manual 4-speed
CHASSIS	Channel section
SUSPENSION	Leaf spring front and rear
BRAKES	Bendix cable-operated drum
TOP SPEED	143km/h (89mph)
ACCELERATION	0-96km/h (60mph): 17 seconds

S.S. Jaguar

NINETEEN thirty five was a year of pivotal importance for William Lyons and his young company. Above all, it marked the arrival of the much improved S.S. Jaguar range which benefited from a new overhead-valve version of the Standard-based engine. Here, at last, was a power unit that began to reflect the quality of the cars' coachwork.

No one was more aware than Lyons of the limitations of the inefficient side-valve engines on which he relied. His salvation came in the outspoken form of the London-based tuning specialist Harry Weslake, who suggested that he create an overhead-valve cylinder head to be grafted on to the 2.6 litre Standard block.

The results were spectacular. Whereas the basic unit had produced 70bhp, Weslake's ministrations generated 103bhp. Lyons was delighted; the figure was 10 per cent better than he had dare hope.

The fitment of this enhanced power unit demanded a new model name and Lyons asked his publicity department to produce a list of animal, bird and fish names. He recalled that 'I immediately pounced on Jaguar as it had an exciting sound to me.' It reminded him of the Armstrong Siddeley Jaguar aero engine of First World War days.

Hitherto S.S. had lacked an engineering department but it arrived in April 1935 in the form of 32-year-old William Munger Heynes (1903-1989), formerly of Humber. He was to become, after William Lyons, the most important individual in the company.

The S.S. Jaguars were announced at the 1935 Motor Show for the 1936 season, although the 2.1 litre model was dropped and a 1.5 litre car, announced as the S.S.II in 1932, retained its side valves.

The benefits of the new cylinder head were immediately apparent. The '2.5 litre' was a respectable

Left: A 1938 S.S. Jaguar 2.5 litre drophead coupé with performance enhanced by an overhead-valve engine. At £415, it cost £20 more than the saloon. This model replaced the S.S.1 four-seater tourer that was discontinued in 1937.

Above: A 1938 3.5 litre drophead coupé. Below: The smallest model in the S.S. Jaguar range and the last to benefit from Harry Weslake's overhead-valve cylinder head was this '1.5 litre' all-steel saloon – capacity was, in fact, 1776cc!

8km/h (5mph) faster, at 137km/h (85mph), and more accelerative than its predecessor. The smaller model acquired its overhead valves for 1938 and the same year came a supplementary 3.5 litre ohv unit which had rather more S.S. than Standard in it.

In 1935, the year of the S.S. Jaguar's arrival, the firm's name changed from Swallow Coach-building to S.S. Cars. After a mere four years as a motor manufacturer William Lyons clearly meant business!

SPECIFICATION	S.S. JAGUAR (2.5 litre)
ENGINE	Straight 6, 2663cc
HORSEPOWER	102bhp @ 4600rpm
TRANSMISSION	Manual 4-speed
CHASSIS	Channel section partially boxed
SUSPENSION	Leaf spring front and rear
BRAKES	Girling rod-operated drum
TOP SPEED	137km/h (85mph)
ACCELERATION	0-96km/h (60mph): 17.4 seconds

S.S. *Jaguar 100*

THE S.S. 90 sports car came of age in 1936 when it became the S.S. Jaguar 100 on receipt of the 2.6 litre overhead-valve engine developed for the saloons. This pushed its top speed towards the 153km/h (95mph) mark. In 1938 came the 3.5 litre six, and in this form it breached the magic 161km/h (100mph), for a selling price of just £445.

The 100 sports car arrived with the S.S. Jaguar saloon at the 1935 Motor Show. Styling was essentially that of the 90 two-seater but there were some important differences below the surface. Whilst the chassis had S.S.1 ancestry, the improved suspension and steering were courtesy of the mainstream cars.

So called because the engine developed an impressive 104bhp, this handsome two-seater was destined to remain available in 2.5 litre form until 1939.

It soon became popular in sprints, rallies and club events although in competition it tended to be overshadowed by the larger 3.5 litre version.

The arrival of this six for the 1938 saloons resulted in the definitive 100, outwardly similar with the well established heavily louvred bonnet, long flowing wings and cutaway doors, but now with

All pictures: The 3.5 litre 100, the definitive S.S. sports car, which offered the established Lyons formula of looks combined with performance at reasonable cost. This was the company's first 161km/h (100mph) production car and this example dates from 1939. Despite the 3.5 litre six being available from 1938, the earlier 2.5 unit could still be specified.

SPECIFICATION	S.S. JAGUAR 100 (3.5 litre)
ENGINE	Straight 6, 3485cc
HORSEPOWER	125bhp @ 4250rpm
TRANSMISSION	Manual 4-speed
CHASSIS	Channel section partially boxed
SUSPENSION	Leaf spring front and rear
BRAKES	Girling rod-operated drum
TOP SPEED	163km/h (101mph)
ACCELERATION	0-96km/h (60mph): 10.4 seconds

performance to match. Top speed was 163km/h (101mph) and 96km/h (60mph) was reached in less than 11 seconds.

When *The Autocar* came to road test an example in 1938, it enthusiastically proclaimed: 'S.S. Cars have certainly produced a machine to covet, and a star performer, particularly in acceleration. This is all the more remarkable at a price well below £500. Not least, it is of satisfying appearance.' Here, in essence, was the Lyons philosophy!

Brakes, steering and road holding also came in for praise, whilst the 100 could attain 128km/h (80mph) in third gear and was remarkably flexible in top.

Once again actively campaigned by enthusiastic amateurs, there was a first and second overall, manufacturers' team prize and a class success in the 1937 RAC Rally. This was followed by class wins in the 1938 RAC and Welsh events.

Although S.S.100 production ceased in 1939, one car spent the war in the stables of Lyons' home, Wappenbury Hall, near Leamington Spa. It was sold, after hostilities, to Ian Appleyard, who won the 1948 Alpine Rally in it, which proved to be the first of his many Coupes des Alpes awards.

Jaguar Mark V

THE MARK V of 1948 was outwardly a pre-war styled saloon, yet it cloaked a modern independent-front-suspension chassis created for a new but unannounced model.

In 1945 S.S. became Jaguar Cars and, like many other manufacturers, reintroduced its pre-war range, with the exception of the S.S. 100 sports car that was dropped. These 1.5, 2.5 and 3.5 litre models were produced until 1948 when they made way for the Mark V. At this point, the smallest capacity engine was discontinued.

Jaguar had already completed designs for a luxurious 161km/h (100mph) saloon which was to be powered by a new twin-overhead-camshaft engine. Similarly chief engineer Heynes had also created a chassis for what was unveiled as the Mark VII in 1950.

But whilst both of these components were ready to enter production, there were delays in Pressed Steel completing a new body shell. What the company required was a stop gap model, hence the Mark V, produced between 1948 and 1951.

This was, to all intents and purposes, the pre-war 2.5/3.5 litre saloon, restyled and updated with faired-in headlamps and press-button door handles. But beneath the surface was a new box-section chassis with torsion bar independent-front-suspension and hydraulic brakes.

The Mark V perpetuated its predecessor's sixes. As such it was the last pushrod-engined Jaguar, but by this time Foleshill had taken over their manufacture. The company had been offered the engine plant by Standard which was to concentrate its post-war production on the single Vanguard model.

Lyons wasted little time in producing a cheque and transferring the machine tools, fearing that Standard's Sir John Black (knighted in 1943), an unpredictable individual, would change his mind. He did but by then it was too late!

Produced mostly in saloon form – there were also some drophead coupés – the Mark V was a well mannered, traditional model produced at a time when there was a strong demand for transport.

By the time that the last example left the Coventry factory in June 1951, 10,466 examples had been built. But by then the long awaited Mark VII, the first generation of post-war saloons, had entered production and Jaguar was really motoring.

SPECIFICATION	JAGUAR MARK V (2.5 litre)
ENGINE	Straight 6, 2663cc
HORSEPOWER	102bhp @ 4600rpm
TRANSMISSION	Manual 4-speed
CHASSIS	Box section
SUSPENSION	Independent front, leaf spring rear
BRAKES	Girling hydraulic drum
TOP SPEED	142km/h (88mph)
ACCELERATION	0-96km/h (60mph): 17.1 seconds

Left: The Jaguar mascot enhancing the radiator of a 1951 3.5 litre Mark V. Below: The Mark V's pre-war lines were updated by the use of faired-in headlamps. This was combined with a new independent front suspension chassis designed for the projected Mark VII. Power still came from Standard-based 2.5 or 3.5 litre, six-cylinder, pushrod engines. The model was built until 1951 and was the last Jaguar saloon to be offered with the option of drophead coupé coachwork. Right: This car retains its original rear wheel spats. The V was also the last Jaguar on which the boot lid pivoted at the base.

19

Jaguar XK 120

JAGUAR'S sports car line, in abeyance since 1939, was dramatically revived in 1948 with the sensational arrival of the XK 120. One of the world's most outstanding performance cars, it found particular favour in America where, with MG, it spearheaded a sports car revival that still endures.

During the Second World War, William Heynes, ably assisted by fellow engineers Walter Hassan and Claude Baily, had designed a 3.4 litre six cylinder engine for a 161km/h (100mph) saloon that Lyons intended to build when peace came.

Adventurously, this XK unit featured a high efficiency hemispherical cylinder head with inclined valves actuated by twin overhead camshafts. It was a configuration that had hitherto been the preserve of racing machinery and costly but often temperamental sports cars.

As already recounted, this model was delayed and the transitional Mark V introduced. In the meantime, the British government was urging the motor industry to export its products to generate much needed foreign currency for an economy decimated by war.

It was against this background that the XK 120 was hastily conceived to share Jaguar's stand at the 1948 Motor Show with the Mark V saloon. Appropriately, both models used a common chassis, with the 120's a shortened version of the V's frame.

But it was perhaps the magnificent open two-seater bodywork that was the most stunning ingredient of the new model. And beneath its

bonnet the XK 120 was the first recipient of Jaguar's new handsome and potent twin-cam six.

The model more than lived up to its looks and the name also reflected the car's top speed. The figure generated some disbelief, so in 1949 the factory prepared a example, standard other than the fitment of a faired cockpit and undershield, that was timed at 224. 64km/h (139.59mph) on the Jabbeke/Ostend autoroute . . .

Demand for the car caught William Lyons by surprise. He had envisaged, at most, a single year's manufacturing life, so the

aluminium body was coachbuilt in the traditional manner. But such was the demand that a switch was made in 1950 to a quantity-produced, pressed steel shell.

The roadster was joined in 1951 by an elegant fixed head coupé version which was followed by a drophead model in 1953. In 1955 came its XK 140 successor, so ensuring the success of a line that would endure until 1961.

SPECIFICATION	JAGUAR XK 120
ENGINE	Straight 6, 3442cc
HORSEPOWER	160bhp @ 5000rpm
TRANSMISSION	Manual 4-speed
CHASSIS	Box section
SUSPENSION	Independent front, leaf spring rear
BRAKES	Lockheed hydraulic drum
TOP SPEED	200km/h (124mph)
ACCELERATION	0-96km/h (60mph): 10 seconds

Below: A 1954 XK 120 drophead coupé, the rarest of the 120 models with 1765 built, with its well-cut horsehair-padded roof raised. It had proper wind-up windows, which resulted in a very snug cabin that even included an interior light.

21

Above: The lovely XK 120 coupé also from 1954. This example has been restored to racing specifications.
Below: The coupé's fixed roof meant that the interior could benefit from a fine walnut-veneered dashboard.

The XK 120 was the first Jaguar to be powered by the company's legendary 3.4 litre, twin-overhead-camshaft XK engine. This left-hand-drive 1949 car is one of the 240, produced between July 1949 and May 1950, to be fitted with aluminium bodywork. As a result, these cars are much sought after by collectors. Subsequent examples used outwardly similar pressed steel hulls; the model was built until 1954. No less than 85 per cent of 120s were exported, the vast majority of these going to America.

The disc wheels featured on this car were the standard fitment; wire wheels were available at extra cost. Note that the instrument panel is leather-covered, unlike the walnut dash of the coupé on the previous page. The 120 caused a sensation at the 1948 London Motor Show; it looked good then and still does today.

Jaguar Mark VII

JAGUAR'S long awaited 161km/h (100mph) saloon finally appeared at the 1950 Motor Show. This large car, powered by the XK six which had been designed for it, was thus the company's first twin-cam-engined, closed model.

In truth the Mark VII was far more suited to the American market than the British one and it comes as no surprise to find that it was, in the first instance, only available for export, particularly to the USA. There its long legs were in sympathy with the terrain and a petrol consumption of some 17 litres/100km (16mpg) was positively economical by trans-Atlantic standards!

The Mark VII therefore replaced the Mark V family, there being no Mark VI Jaguar because Bentley was already using the designation.

The public was already familiar with two aspects of the VII's specifications because its chassis had already proved its worth on the Mark V and the XK 120 had been a perfect vehicle for publicising the virtues of the 3.4 litre twin-cam six.

It was soon after the VII entered production that Jaguar moved from Foleshill, its home since 1928. Such had been the company's growth that it was outstripping the confines of the Holbrook Lane site. In 1951 the transfer began, some 3km (2 miles) to the west, to a former Daimler wartime aero engine factory on the outskirts of Coventry. The

SPECIFICATION	JAGUAR MARK VII
ENGINE	Straight 6, 3442cc
HORSEPOWER	160bhp @ 5200rpm
TRANSMISSION	Manual 4-speed
CHASSIS	Box section
SUSPENSION	Independent front, leaf spring rear
BRAKES	Girling hydraulic
TOP SPEED	163km/h (101mph)
ACCELERATION	0-96km/h (60mph) 13.7 seconds

move was completed late in 1952 and Browns Lane, Allesley has been Jaguar's home ever since.

As announced the Mark VII employed its predecessor's gearbox, but in 1953 the demands of the American market required automatic transmission and Jaguar responded by offering an optional two speed Borg-Warner unit.

Some 21,000 examples had been built by the time that the model developed as the VIIM in 1955 with engine power boosted from 160 to 190bhp. This was produced for two years and, in 1957, was replaced by the Mark VIII, instantly identifiable by its curved windscreen that replaced a two-piece divided one.

In 1959 came the last of the series; the Mark IX was the first Jaguar saloon to benefit from an enlarged 3.8 litre race-bred version of the XK engine with competition-honed, all-round disc brakes and power-assisted steering.

By the time that the IX was replaced by the Mark X in 1961, it was an ageing concept but, along with the XK 120, it had helped to establish Jaguar as a truly international car company.

Left: The commodious Mark VII saloon, this is a 1951 example, for which the XK engine was designed. It was a line that was to endure until 1961. The divided two-piece windscreen would be a feature until the arrival of the Mark VIII. Above: The well-appointed driving compartment with the speedometer in front of the driver and the revolution counter tucked away to the left. A tool kit was conveniently located in each of the substantial front doors. Walnut veneers were used extensively throughout the interior.
Right: The Mark VII was not offered with a mascot, that would have to wait for the VIII; instead, it featured this stylized jaguar head.

Jaguar C-Type

JAGUAR'S first purpose-designed sports racing car, the C-Type, achieved a spectacular first-time-out victory at Le Mans in 1951, giving Britain its first triumph in the 24 hour classic since 1935. The cars were similarly successful in 1953.

In the 1950 event, Jaguar had unofficially sponsored a trio of XK 120s and although two finished in 12th and 15th places respectively, the remaining car withdrew at the 21st hour whilst lying third.

William Heynes and Jaguar's racing manager 'Lofty' England returned from France convinced that a purpose-designed car, powered by the reliable and potent XK twin-cam engine, could be victorious.

For Lyons, the attraction was that Le Mans was the world's most famous motor race and a victory there would generate enormous publicity for sales of his all-important saloons.

With this in mind, in October 1950 he gave his approval for the construction of a team of sports racing cars that could run in the 1951 event. The intention was to produce a more powerful, lighter version of the XK 120 and so the XK 120C, for Competition, was born.

Whilst Heynes proceeded with the design of of a multi-tubular space-frame chassis, aero-dynamicist Malcolm Sayer, who in 1950 had joined Jaguar from the Bristol Aeroplane Company, was responsible for the bodywork.

Below: The ultimate C-Type with all-round disc brakes. This is the restored car that won at Le Mans in 1953.

The 233km/h (145mph) cars were completed just in time for the 1951 race and although two dropped out, the third, driven by Peter Walker and Peter Whitehead, won.

To run as it did in the prototype class, a minimum of 50 cars had to be built, so the C-Type was offered for general sale at £2327 which was £650 more than the production XK 120.

However, Jaguar was less lucky in 1952 when eleventh hour modifications to the cars' noses resulted in overheating and the entire team withdrew.

But the Coventry company was back again in 1953 with C-Types that more closely resembled their 1951 forebears although they were lighter, aided by the use of thinner-gauge chassis tubing and flexible aircraft-style petrol tanks. Innovative all-round disc brakes, developed in conjunction with Dunlop, were employed.

This time there was no mistake. Not only did the entire team finish but they took first, second and fourth places. The Jaguar racing legend was in the making.

SPECIFICATION	JAGUAR C-TYPE
ENGINE	Straight 6, 3442cc
HORSEPOWER	200bhp @ 5800rpm
TRANSMISSION	Manual 4-speed
CHASSIS	Tubular space frame
SUSPENSION	Independent front, live rear axle
BRAKES	Lockheed hydraulic drum
TOP SPEED	230km/h (143mph)
ACCELERATION	0-96km/h (60mph): 8.1 seconds

Left: The 1953 C-Type's triple twin-choke Weber carburettors, fed by ducted air from the bonnet, contributed to the 3.4 litre XK engine developing an impressive 220bhp, which compared with 160 for the roadgoing XK 120.

Below: XKC 051, one of three lightweight cars, in which Tony Rolt and Duncan Hamilton won the 1953 Le Mans race. It was Jaguar's second victory in the race. It is currently owned by Adrian Hamilton, son of the late Duncan.

27

Jaguar D-Type

UNQUESTIONABLY the most famous of the sports racing Jaguars, the D-Type provided the company with no less than three victories at Le Mans. In addition to this impressive record, it also marked the genesis of Jaguar's legendary E-Type sports car.

Although C-Types had swept the board in 1953, the design was beginning to become outdated and that autumn William Heynes began work on a replacement. Once again the intention was to reduce weight, increase engine power and improve aerodynamics.

To these ends, the tubular chassis was replaced by an extended monocoque cockpit of riveted aluminium alloy sheet with the engine and front suspension attached to a framework of square-section magnesium tubing. However, the 3.4 litre engine was essentially that of the C, with output boosted to 240bhp.

The open body was completely new and surmounted on the driver's side by a shapely stabilizing fin. Malcolm Sayer had once again woven his magic and the result was one of the most visually impressive and memorable competition cars of all time.

A team of three were completed in time for the 1954 Le Mans race but they were unable to challenge a 4.9 litre Ferrari, which won. Although a D-Type came in second place, the two others dropped out.

More power was clearly needed and the XK's output was upped to 270bhp whilst Sayer redesigned and lengthened the D's nose to increase airflow.

These improved D's ran at Le Mans in 1955, an event that was overshadowed by a crash that killed 81 people. The Mercedes-Benz team withdrew and a D-Type, driven by Mike Hawthorn and Ivor Bueb, won with the Belgian-entered D-Type third.

Similar cars entered in 1956, two crashed and one came in sixth, but a D-Type entered by the Edinburgh-based Ecurie Ecosse team, won. It was at this high point that Jaguar decided to withdraw from competition.

Below: Classic lines by Jaguar's Malcolm Sayer. This is the 1955 D-Type XKD 504, first of the 'long-nosed' cars.

Right: Rear view of the same long-nosed D-Type, a works car and the spare at Le Mans in 1955. Although this is a two-seater, the passenger's compartment was, in the interests of aerodynamics, covered by a cowl. The distinctive tail fin also houses the petrol filler cap.

The factory did, however, provide unofficial support for Ecurie Ecosse in the 1957 race and two of its cars, with enlarged 3.8 litre engines, came in first and second. French and Belgian privateers were third and fourth respectively.

This completed the string of Jaguar victories in the 1950s with five wins in seven years. The last occasion that a British make had so dominated the race had been in the 1920s when the ultra reliable Bentleys trounced the Continental opposition. Now that coveted accolade had passed to Jaguar.

29

Left: D-Types are highly prized today and possess the allure that was apparent in the 1950s when their Le Mans victories made them world-famous. Racing driver Mike Salmon drives John Coombs' car at the 1993 Goodwood Festival of Speed.

SPECIFICATION	JAGUAR D-TYPE
ENGINE	Straight 6, 3442cc
HORSEPOWER	250bhp @ 5750rpm
TRANSMISSION	Manual 4-speed
CHASSIS	Monocoque centre section
SUSPENSION	Independent front, live rear axle
BRAKES	Dunlop disc
TOP SPEED	261km/h (162mph)
ACCELERATION	0-96km/h (60mph): 4.7 seconds

All pictures: This is one of the production D-Types; Jaguar were required to build 50 replicas of its racers to meet Le Mans regulations – although not all manufacturers did! They outwardly resemble the works cars but were not originally fitted with a stabilizing fin, although many have acquired one over the years. This D-Type, XKD 527, was dispatched to America in November 1955. It is thought to have been the first D to have been imported into California. The first owner was Jerry Austin of Arcadia, and the car was road-tested by Road and Track *magazine. Driven by Sherwood Johnson, it was placed first in the 1956 Torrey Pines One Hour Road Race.*

Jaguar XKSS

LIKE THE C-Type, the D was also offered for public sale but demand was limited. Early in 1957 Jaguar launched a road-equipped version of the design which it called the XKSS.

By the end of 1956, the firm had no less than 29 unsold D-Types in stock, but from the other side of the Atlantic the Sports Car Club of America intimated that the D would be eligible for production sports car racing there. With the United States Jaguar's largest market, this opportunity could not be ignored and so the XKSS, probably standing for Super Sports rather than any pre-war associations, was born.

Here was the ultimate but wildly impractical road car, a 241km/h (150mph) open two-seater, about as closely related to a Le Mans winner as you could get. Nevertheless, a few modifications were necessary to convert this sports racer for the road.

This necessitated the fitment of a high wrap-around windscreen in place of the original and a rudimentary hood was provided. For racing there had only been a driver's door whilst the space for a non-existent passenger was covered by a cowl. This was removed and a seat introduced, along with a small nearside door. Below it was a plated and drilled shield to protect the occupants from the raucous exhaust pipe which emerged just ahead of the rear wheel arch. The XKSS was not a car for the faint hearted!

There was no boot, the space being occupied by the spare wheel and twin flexible 165 litres (36.5

gallon) petrol tanks, so a chromium-plated rack was attached to the tail for the proverbial suitcase. Bumpers were fitted all round.

As might be expected, performance was electrifying, as virtually no changes had been made to the 3.4 litre triple-carburettored, dry sump engine. The magic 161km/h (100mph) came up in under 14 seconds which was about twice the figure for the contemporary XK 140.

Sales began in January 1957 but at £3878 there were few takers and the model's prospects were not helped by a fire that broke out at Browns Lane on 12th February which destroyed about half the works.

XKSS production restarted in March but the model was only destined to survive until November, by which time just 16 examples had been delivered. Of these, no less than 12 were exported to America and Canada.

So ended the XKSS. However, during 1957, work had begun on a proper roadgoing version of the D, although it would be another four years before the E-Type finally took to the road.

33

Left: This 1957 XKSS, the D-Type for the road, is identifiable by its full-width windscreen, hood, shielded exhaust pipes and luggage rack. Above: The triple-Weber-carburettored, 3.4 litre, dry sump engine differed little from the competition D-Type unit, although it was possible to fit a larger fan pulley for the dynamo. The forward-opening bonnet meant that engine accessibility was particularly good. Right: The speedometer reads to 180mph (290km/h) and the rev counter to 8000rpm. The cockpit required the fitment of a passenger seat and a cubbyhole was introduced. The trim quality was also superior to that of the D-Type.

SPECIFICATION	JAGUAR XKSS
ENGINE	Straight 6, 3442cc
HORSEPOWER	250bhp @ 5750rpm
TRANSMISSION	Manual 4-speed
CHASSIS	Monocoque cockpit
SUSPENSION	Independent front, live rear axle
BRAKES	Dunlop disc
TOP SPEED	240km/h (149mph)
ACCELERATION	0-96km/h (60mph): 5.2 seconds

Jaguar Mark I

Below: The Jaguar mascot is seen here on a 1957 Mark I saloon. This is a 3.4 litre version of the model which featured a new, enlarged radiator grille with narrower slats.

IN 1956 Jaguar was still a relatively small company and built some 12,000 cars. A decade later, in 1966, output had more than doubled to close on 26,000 units and corporate profits risen fourfold to over £1.5 million.

This impressive performance was, in the main, due to one model, a sporting medium-sized saloon which first appeared in 1956 and endured, in essence, until 1969.

When the big Mark VII saloon appeared in 1950, it effectively replaced the 3.5 litre Mark V, but the 2.5 litre version was not perpetuated. This omission was remedied in 1956 when Jaguar announced a model located between the two-plus-two XK 140 sports car and the VII.

Once again the versatile XK engine was employed although this time it appeared in a new capacity of 2483cc. Prior to its arrival, all Jaguars had retained a separate chassis but the new car reflected current design trends in being the company's first unitary construction model.

Above all, its sleek appearance and rounded contours ensured that the 2.4 could not be mistaken for any car other than a Jaguar. Inside, there were the customary trimmings, walnut veneers evident on the dashboard and door fillets and well upholstered leather seats.

In its original form the 2.4 was capable of a respectable, if not particularly accelerative 161km/h (100mph), and soon owners, particularly in America, were yearning for more performance.

SPECIFICATION	JAGUAR MARK I (2.4 litre)
ENGINE	Straight 6, 2483cc
HORSEPOWER	112bhp @ 5750rpm
TRANSMISSION	Manual 4-speed
CHASSIS	Unitary construction
SUSPENSION	Independent front, leaf-spring rear
BRAKES	Lockheed hydraulic drum
TOP SPEED	163km/h (101mph)
ACCELERATION	0-96km/h (60mph): 14.4 seconds

This arrived in 1957 in the form of a supplementary 3.4 litre version, which was instantly identifiable by a new wider radiator grille, similar to that used on the XK 150 sports car. Performance immediately soared to around the 193km/h (120mph) mark. Later, in 1958, it was arrested by the option of all-round disc brakes.

The car ceased production in 1960 after close on 27,000 examples of both capacity engines had been produced. This compares with some 16,000 Mark VIII/IXs built over the same period which reveals the importance of these comfortably sized saloons in the fortunes of Jaguar Cars.

The 2.4/3.4 models were replaced by the much improved Mark II family whereupon the original retrospectively became the Mark I. A line that had begun in 1956 was about to attain a new lease of life.

Below: The 3.4 litre Mark I, with optional wire wheels. The cutaway, as opposed to the full, rear wheel spats of the 2.4, also identifies the larger engined version.

Jaguar XK 140 & 150

THE FINAL manifestation of the 120 sports car line and its fastest representative, the XK 150, which appeared in 1957, was built until 1961.

After the XK 120 had ceased production in 1954, it was succeeded by the XK140 which benefited from the fitment of rack and pinion steering and was identifiable by a thicker slatted radiator grille and larger bumpers. This endured until 1957 when it was replaced by the XK 150.

It was the beneficiary of an ingenious facelift which resulted in a higher wing line and featured a wider radiator grille. Once again, the 3.4 litre XK engine was employed but in 1959 it was supplemented by the 3.8 litre unit which had already appeared in the Mark VIII saloon.

Both engines were available with a choice of cylinder heads which reflected Jaguar's successful racing programme. In addition to the standard head, there was the more powerful B type and the top line, 'straight port', triple-carburettored S.

Specified with competition proven discs, XK 150s were usually shod with wire wheels available at extra cost.

Originally available in two-plus-two fixed and drophead coupé forms, a two-seater roadster with wind-up windows, rather than the 140's sidescreens, did not arrive until 1958. It was similarly available with the same choices of engine and states of tune.

Below: A 1958 XK 140 coupé. Usually disc wheels were fitted, but these wires were available as an option.

This ensured than the 150 was still a potent performer. In 3.4 litre S guise, the open car was capable of over 217km/h (135mph) and 96km/h (60mph) came up in a little over seven seconds.

But the reality was that the concept was beginning to age. Like people, cars tend to put on weight as they get older and, at 1447kg (3192lb) in open form, the 150 was some 127kg (280lb) heavier than its XK 120 equivalent of 10 years before.

Over 9000 examples were built, which was around 1000 more than its XK 140 predecessor. Once again it was America that took the vast majority of cars with over 80 per cent of production crossing the Atlantic.

However, these figures did not match the 120, which was by far and away the most successful model of the line, with over 12,000 finding owners. Yet even these figures were to be overwhelmed by the astounding success of the E-Type that replaced the XK 150 in 1961.

Above: A 1957 XK 150 fixed head coupé.
Right: A 1960 3.4 litre XK 150 donhead coupé.

SPECIFICATION	JAGUAR XK 150S (3.8 litre)
ENGINE	Straight 6, 3781cc
HORSEPOWER	265bhp @ 5500rpm
TRANSMISSION	Manual 4-speed
CHASSIS	Box section
SUSPENSION	Independent front, leaf spring rear
BRAKES	Dunlop disc
TOP SPEED	219km/h (136mph)
ACCELERATION	0-96km/h (60mph): 7.6 seconds

Jaguar Mark II

THE COMPACT Jaguar saloon line, begun in 1956 with the 2.4 litre model, flowered as the Mark II in 1959. A great visual and mechanical improvement on the original, it survived in this form until 1969.

As Jaguar's first unitary construction saloon the 2.4 was, in retrospect, an overstrong structure, a familiar outcome for any car company adopting this new technology.

Thankfully, the Mark II reflected a more assured approach with the result that the thicker, rather inelegant door and windscreen pillars of the original model were slimmed down. The result was a more visually pleasing body with a much larger area of glass than the original. A new radiator grille with a distinctive central rib completed the revisions.

Mechanical refinements included an increase in the width of the live rear axle to the benefit of roadholding and all-round Dunlop disc brakes were now standard.

The number of engine options rose to three with the arrival of the 3.8 litre unit at the top of the range to join the 2.4 and 3.4 sixes already on offer.

The 201km/h (125mph) 3.8 Mark II was a potent, if thirsty car, and was essential transport for aspiring bank robbers if the B-movies of the day are to be believed! The optional wire-spoked wheels were similarly very desirable.

Likewise popular with police forces at a time when an increasing number of motorways were being opened, the Mark II's ultra reliable XK engine

Below: The lines of the much improved Mark II saloon; this is a 3.8 litre example, with optional wire wheels. It was the fastest Jaguar road car of its day.

SPECIFICATION	JAGUAR MARK II (3.4 litre)
ENGINE	Straight 6, 3442cc
HORSEPOWER	210bhp @ 5500rpm
TRANSMISSION	Manual 4-speed
CHASSIS	Unitary construction
SUSPENSION	Independent front, leaf spring rear
BRAKES	Dunlop disc
TOP SPEED	193km/h (120mph)
ACCELERATION	0-96km/h (60mph): 11.9 seconds

The arrival for 1968 of Jaguar's new XJ6 saloon saw the Mark II downgraded, with the 2.4 renamed the 240. It was built until 1969 whilst the 3.4 litre 340 was only available in 1968.

Mention should also be made of the Mark II-based Daimler V8 250. Jaguar had bought the old established Coventry company in 1960 and this hybrid was outwardly similar to the Jaguar, apart from the fitment of its fluted but badgeless radiator grille.

This 1963 model was powered by the 2.5 litre V8 engine, hitherto used in the Daimler SP250 sports car. The V8 250 also ceased production when the 240 saloon was discontinued in 1969.

proved itself well able to sustain long periods of high speed motoring.

At the other extreme the 2.4 was a 153km/h (95mph) car, whilst the 3.4 could attain 193km/h (120mph). These well equipped, comfortable sports saloons were by far and away the most popular Jaguar of the 1960s.

Below: A 1968 240 Mark II in company with its 1967 Daimler stablemate (right). This used the Mark II's bodyshell but with Daimler's 2.5 litre V8. Automatic transmission was fitted but a manual gearbox was offered from 1967.

Above: The Mark II benefited from a larger glass area than the Mark I. This included the rear window, that was of the semi-wraparound type, so that it nearly met the rear quarterlights of the back doors.

39

Jaguar E-Type Coupé

MARCH 16th 1961 is one of the most famous dates in Jaguar chronology. It was then that the 31st Geneva Motor Show opened its doors to the public and there could be little doubt that the star of the event was Jaguar's new 241km/h (150mph) E-Type sports car which was unveiled in coupé form.

Despite the acclaim accorded to the E-Type, Sir William Lyons had a curiously ambivalent attitude to the model, perhaps because it would never sell in the same numbers as his saloons. This may, however, explain its long gestation period of an existing design which was in excess of four years.

But of the two E-Type bodies, he much preferred the closed version which was accorded the GT, for Grand Tourer, designation. At £2196, it was £99 more expensive than the roadster.

Like the open car, it was an uncompromising two-seater but there was a roomy luggage platform with access accorded by an opening rear door. It was also marginally faster than the roadster because the greater weight was more than offset by the aerodynamic superiority of a closed body over an open one.

More popular in Britain than in the mainstream American market, the model benefited from 4.2 litre power in 1965 and was joined in 1966 by a two-plus-two version which was only available in closed form.

This was 228mm (9in) longer than the original car to permit the introduction of two additional rear seats, although, in truth, these were more suitable for children than adults. When not in use the squabs could be folded forward to provide additional carrying space.

These alterations required a higher roof line to the detriment of the original design. Despite this aesthetic compromise, the model proved popular with the family man who still wanted to enjoy his performance motoring.

Like the roadster, the E-Type coupé was also built in Series II form from late 1968 and this also applied to the two-plus-two. However, the latter model was available with automatic transmission created for the important American market, although the concept flew somewhat in the face of the sports car ideal.

Both closed cars were discontinued when the Series II models were replaced by the V12-powered roadster and coupé E-Types in 1971 which perpetuated the two-plus-two's longer wheelbase.

Below: The Series II E-Type appeared for the 1969 season.

SPECIFICATION	JAGUAR E-TYPE (4.2 litre)
ENGINE	Straight 6, 4235cc
HORSEPOWER	265bhp @ 5400rpm
TRANSMISSION	Manual 4-speed
CHASSIS	Monocoque cockpit
SUSPENSION	Independent front and rear
BRAKES	Dunlop disc
TOP SPEED	241km/h (150mph)
ACCELERATION	0-96km/h (60mph): 7 seconds

Left: A series II E-Type dashboard, with instrument panel conforming to American safety regulations, with rocker switches replacing the previous toggles. Below: A 1968 4.2 litre Series II in the foreground with a 1969 model in the background.

Jaguar E-Type Roadster

JUST 15 days after the coupé version of the E-Type appeared at Geneva, the roadster was unveiled at the New York Motor Show that opened on 1st April. This choice of location was a reflection of the fact that the open car would be more popular on the other side of the Atlantic than the closed one. And so it proved.

The international acclaim accorded to the Le Mans-winning D-Type made a road-going version both desirable and inevitable. In retrospect, the XKSS of 1957 can be viewed as an unfortunate eccentricity but, by then, work had already started on the design of a replacement for the ageing XK line.

William Heynes essentially adopted the approach that he had applied to the D. This was based on a monocoque tub with triangulated framework at the front to carry the 3.8 litre XK engine in XK 150 triple-carburettored S guise. Inevitably, this substructure was executed in steel rather than the D's lighter but costly magnesium alloy.

The sports racer had retained a live rear axle but the E was to benefit from an all-independent unit developed for Jaguar's new Mark X saloon that replaced the IX later in 1961.

When it came to the car's line, aerodynamicist Malcolm Sayer lavished his formidable talents to produce a shape clearly derived from the D-Type that must rank as one of the most accomplished and memorable in the history of the motor car.

Little wonder that the model, in both roadster and coupé forms, was an instant head-turner. It still is today.

As the E-Type was some 227kg (500 lb) lighter than the XK 150, its performance was superior to it. Although Jaguar claimed a top speed of 241km/h (150mph), the truth was that only the handful of carefully assembled press cars were capable of the figure. However, most 3.8 litre E-Types could comfortably exceed the 225km/h (140mph) mark.

The roadster was built in its original form until late in 1964 when the model received a 4.2 litre engine. In 1969 a Series II version of the E-Type appeared with exposed headlights, heavier bumpers and cockpit refinements in order to conform with all-important American safely regulations.

Below: The Series I E-Type roadster with headlamps contained behind perspex covers, small air intake and narrow bumpers. This is a 1962 3.8 litre car.

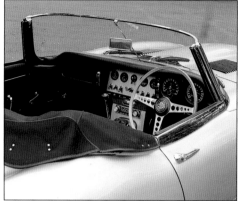

Left: Looking good from any angle, with twin exhaust pipes making a contribution to the back. Above: The driving compartment with a memorable view down the bonnet.

43

This was built until 1971 when six cylinder E-Type production ceased to make way for the V12-powered Series III cars. By this time a total of 57,220 examples had been built, of which some 60 per cent were roadsters, making the E-Type by far and away the most successful and memorable of all Jaguar sports cars.

SPECIFICATION	JAGUAR E-TYPE (3.8 litre)
ENGINE	Straight 6, 3781cc
HORSEPOWER	260bhp @ 5500rpm
TRANSMISSION	Manual 4-speed
CHASSIS	Monocoque cockpit
SUSPENSION	Independent front and rear
BRAKES	Dunlop disc
TOP SPEED	240km/h (149mph)
ACCELERATION	0-96km/h (60mph): 7.1 seconds

Far left and below: The E-Type's 3.8 litre engine was replaced by a 4.2 litre unit in October 1964. This Series I roadster is powered by this larger capacity engine and dates from that year. Top speed remained the same although acceleration was improved. A further refinement came with the simultaneous arrival of an all-synchromesh gearbox and brake servo, which was an improvement on the earlier unit. Left: Outwardly the bigger-bored, twin-cam six was indistinguishable from its predecessor. Like the D, engine accessibility was excellent because of the forward-opening bonnet.

Jaguar Mark X

JAGUAR'S large saloon line was updated in 1961 with the arrival of the Mark X. Excessively wide and thirsty, it was not perhaps the happiest of car designs but, like its smaller Mark II stablemate, it did improve as it got older.

Announced in October 1961, seven months after the E-Type, the Mark X with its distinctive quadruple headlamps was as up to date as its Mark IX predecessor had become antiquated. A massive four-door, unitary construction, five-seater saloon, at 1930mm (6ft 4in) wide, it was the the broadest car on the British market.

The Mark X's triple-carburettored, 3.8 litre engine was very similar to that used in the sports car. Likewise, it was the beneficiary of Jaguar's new independent rear suspension system that had been under development principally for a saloon application since 1955. All-round disc brakes were employed.

In truth, such a large car looked more in place on American than British roads and power steering, a popular trans-Atlantic fitment, was provided as standard. Similarly the overwhelming majority of Mark Xs were fitted with automatic transmission.

The car's top speed was nudging the 193km/h (120mph) mark but at the expense of a petrol consumption which was in the region of 20 litres/ 100km (14mpg).

Like the E-Type, the Mark X received the enlarged 4.2 litre engine, and its accompanying all synchromesh gearbox for the manual versions, in 1964. Improvements were also made to the power steering system and the model remained available in this form until 1966.

There was some cross-pollination with the smaller Jaguar saloons when, in 1964, the S-Type appeared. It was a combination of the Mark II front and Mark X rear ends with the options of 3.4 or 3.8 litre power units. This subsequently evolved into the 420 of 1967 with quad headlamps, so named because of its 4.2 litre engine. It resembled a scaled-down Mark X.

Simultaneously, the X proper became the 420G and this lasted until 1970. By this time it had made way for the superlative XJ6 which represented a merging of Jaguar's compact and large car lines.

However, the 420G's substructure was to survive for a further 22 years as it formed the basis of the formal in-house Daimler Limousine. This was the last Browns Lane product to be powered by the XK engine, which was discontinued at the end of 1992.

Below left: The familiar Jaguar mascot was fitted to the Mark X from the outset but was discontinued on its 420G successor in 1968, in deference to American safety regulations. Right: The X's well appointed driving compartment. Automatic transmission was a popular option while power steering was fitted as standard. Below: A Mark X of 3.8 litres. This American-orientated model represented the last of Jaguar's large saloon line, which began in 1938 and survived, in essence, until 1970.

SPECIFICATION	JAGUAR MARK X (4.2 litre)
ENGINE	Straight 6, 4235cc
HORSEPOWER	265bhp @ 5400rpm
TRANSMISSION	Automatic 3-speed
CHASSIS	Unitary construction
SUSPENSION	Independent front and rear
BRAKES	Dunlop disc
TOP SPEED	196km/h (122mph)
ACCELERATION	0-96km/h (60mph): 10.4 seconds

47

Jaguar Low Drag Coupé

DESPITE being derived from the Le Mans-winning D-Type, the E-Type was not a racing car, although the factory did build a limited number of lightened examples for competition. The rarest of these is what aerodynamicist Malcolm Sayer called the Low Drag Coupé that was completed in 1962.

It was at the beginning of the year that Jaguar chassis engineer Derrick White had proposed that the company produce a team of cars to compete in the projected World Manufacturers' Championship which was to be run for Grand Tourers (which are closed cars).

As it transpired, the authorities changed their minds and only one of these special E-Type coupés was built. Like the C, D and E-Types, its body was the work of Sayer who, as ever, was faced with the twin objectives of improving aerodynamics and saving weight. As already mentioned, the former discipline can be more successful applied to a closed car than an open one.

In the interests of weight saving, the body panels of the Low Drag Coupé, which differed visibly from the production closed E-Type, were of aluminium although a steel monocoque hull was employed.

By contrast, the engine was a radical departure from standard, in that it had an alloy block that had featured on the experimental Jaguar, coded E2A. This was related to the E-Type but had appeared at Le Mans, prior to its announcement, in 1960. Originally a 3 litre, it was enlarged to the more orthodox 3.8 litre capacity.

Once completed, the grey painted car was tested from mid-1962 by the Jaguar experimental department. But in the summer of 1963 it was sold to racing driver Dick Protheroe, who registered it CUT 7, having transferred the number from a succession of racing E-Types.

From then until the end of 1964 he actively campaigned it in British and European events. His achievements included a second place and a first in the GT class at Rheims in 1963 and sixth in the TT at Goodwood. The following year he won the GT class in the Paris 1000km event and was placed seventh overall.

Slippery customer; in 1962 Malcolm Sayer produced this single sports racing E-Type in coupé form.

SPECIFICATION	E-TYPE LOW DRAG COUPE
ENGINE	Straight 6, 3781cc
HORSEPOWER	276bhp @ 5750rpm
TRANSMISSION	Manual 4-speed
CHASSIS	Monocoque cockpit
SUSPENSION	Independent front and rear
BRAKES	Dunlop disc
TOP SPEED	249km/h (155mph)
ACCELERATION	N/A

Early in 1965 Protheroe sold the car to David Wansborough who continued to race it for a time, although it later crossed the Atlantic to form part of the collection of historic Jaguars owned by Walter Hill of Florida. It was subsequently returned to Britain and, at the time of writing, this unique car is owned by Viscount Cowdray.

49

Above: The coupé's 3.8 litre aluminium engine was derived from that used in the experimental E2A (right) that ran at Le Mans in 1960. Above right: CUT 7 – the Low Drag Coupé's unique lines shown to advantage here.

'Lightweight' E-Type

Below: One of the Lightweights run by the American Briggs Cunningham in US racing colours and pictured at the 1995 Goodwood Festival of Speed.

DESPITE Jaguar's plans for the E-Type's involvement in the World Manufacturers' Championship being thwarted by changes in the regulations, the factory did produce a limited number of racing versions of the car that were available to selected customers.

Designated by Browns Lane as the 'Special GT E-Type,' they have become more conveniently known as Lightweights.

The first of the breed, which appeared in 1963, was produced for Jaguar distributor John Coombs of Guildford, Surrey. In appearance, it closely resembled the E-Type roadster complete with factory hardtop but, where practicable, alloy parts replaced steel ones.

For the remaining cars this meant the monocoque hull and body panels, and the series was thus more historically allied to its D-Type forebear in this regard. However, the E's more familiar frontal steel triangulated framework was retained.

Changes were also made to the engine which followed those undertaken on the Low Drag Coupé. As such, the Lightweights were powered by an alloy 3.8 litre six, which developed some 300bhp, compared with 265bhp of the production model.

In the first instance it was intended to produce 18 of these cars but, in the event, only 12 were built. Virtually all were delivered in 1963 with the single remaining Lightweight leaving the factory early in 1964.

Eligible for GT racing, they could be bought

SPECIFICATION	LIGHTWEIGHT E-TYPE
ENGINE	Straight 6, 3780cc
HORSEPOWER	296bhp @ 5750rpm
TRANSMISSION	Manual 5-speed
CHASSIS	Alloy monocoque cockpit
SUSPENSION	Independent front and rear
BRAKES	Dunlop disc
TOP SPEED	241km/h (150mph)
ACCELERATION	N/A

American racing driver Briggs Cunningham ran a team of cars at Sebring in 1963, where examples came in seventh and ninth. Of the three Lightweights he entered at Le Mans in 1963, two did not finish but one, driven by Cunningham himself, came in ninth.

Two of the 12 were converted by outside agencies for their owners as closed cars in the manner of the Sayer Low Drag Coupé and one was destroyed by fire.

In truth, whilst the Lightweight E-Types performed reasonably well in short duration British races, in longer European events when faced with the faster, more reliable and lighter Ferrari GTOs, they invariably succumbed.

Currently the surviving Lightweight Es are nurtured by collectors and enthusiasts as testimony to the days when Jaguar's most famous sports car went motor racing.

Below: A sister Cunningham Lightweight. Inset: A 1964 coupé with steel monocoque and aluminium, fuel-injected engine, for wealthy French businessman Pierre Bardinon.

from Jaguar distributors by customers who enjoyed a proven racing record. The first Coombs' Lightweight was driven by such well-known drivers as Graham Hill, Roy Salvadori and Jackie Stewart.

Jaguar XJ13

JAGUAR'S dominance of the Le Mans 24 hour race in the 1950s represents one of the most memorable chapters in the marque's history.

In the following decade, the company once again targeted the event and these ambitions were expressed in the mid-engined XJ13 prototype of 1966. But it never ran there and its existence remained unknown to the general public until 1973!

Powered by Jaguar's long anticipated V12 engine, its origins are rooted in the 1950s, when chief engineer Heynes recognized the limitations of the XK six for racing purposes and proposed a V12 unit in its place. But Jaguar's withdrawal from competition in 1956 meant that the project was set aside.

Below: A skewed dash makes the XJ13 look left-hand-drive!

Above: The mid engined XJ13 as it is today, having been re-built in 1973. The superb styling was by Malcolm Sayer.

Then, in the early 1960s, interest in the 24 hour race was revived at Browns Lane, so the 5 litre V12 unit programme was reactivated and the engine ran for the first time in 1964. By then front-engined sports racers were a thing of the past. Formula 1 became exclusively mid-engined from 1961 and sports racing soon followed suit.

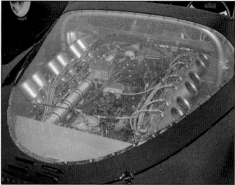

Above: The XJ13's fine 5 litre V12 fuel-injected engine.

SPECIFICATION	JAGUAR XJ13
ENGINE	Mid-located V12, 4993cc
HORSEPOWER	502bhp @ 7600rpm
TRANSMISSION	Manual 5-speed
CHASSIS	Unitary
SUSPENSION	Independent front and rear
BRAKES	Dunlop disc
TOP SPEED	281km/h (175mph)
ACCELERATION	N/A

Jaguar chassis engineer Derrick White, who had been closely involved with the development of the Lightweight E-Types, was responsible for the XJ13's overall concept with Malcolm Sayer once again supervizing body design.

An alloy monocoque structure was employed and the 5 litre V12, with twin overhead camshafts per cylinder bank, was mounted longitudinally behind the driver. The E-Type-related suspension was accordingly all-independent. There were also echoes of that model in the low, lithe, open two-seater bodywork.

The car was completed in March 1966 but despite lapping the Motor Industry Research Association's circuit at 259km/h (161mph), a top speed of 281km/h (175mph) meant that it was not really fast enough to be competitive.

The project was therefore set aside, but in 1971 Jaguar decided to feature the car in a promotional film to launch the V12-engined E-Type, although this roadgoing version used simpler, single overhead camshafts per cylinder bank.

Unfortunately the car crashed whilst it was being tested. Happily, in 1973, the firm decided to rebuild it. Today the XJ13 survives as part of Jaguar's collection of historic cars.

But its appearance was to exert a compelling influence on the next generation of Jaguar stylists, with echoes to be found in the XJ220 supercar and even the latest XK8 coupé.

Jaguar XJ6

UNQUESTIONABLY one of the world's outstanding saloons, the XJ6 of 1968 was destined to survive for 18 years and, such was the excellence of the design, it carried Jaguar through the most traumatic years in its history.

Having merged with the country's largest car maker, the British Motor Corporation, in 1966, two years later Jaguar was drawn into what became British Leyland. This unhappy alliance of almost the entire indigenous motor industry collapsed in 1974 and was then nationalized.

For Jaguar a sense of order was only brought to an increasingly chaotic era in 1980 with John Egan's appointment as its chairman, and this paved the way to a return to the private sector in 1984.

The XJ6 was a replacement for the Mark X and Mark II saloons. Low and sleek, it represented the acme of Sir William Lyons' stylistic talents which were complemented by an outstanding engineering package created by William Heynes and his team. Little wonder the XJ6 was Lyons' all time favourite Jaguar, even though the name itself did not appear anywhere on the car.

The 4.2 litre XK engine was, in essence, carried over from the Mark X although there was also a new 2.8 litre version. A manual gearbox was listed, but the majority of XJ6s were fitted with automatic transmission and power steering was standard.

This description does not begin to do justice to the car's extraordinary levels of refinement,

Left and above: Low and luxurious, the magnificently refined XJ6 saloon, introduced in 1968. This is a 1973 car.

SPECIFICATION	JAGUAR XJ6 (4.2 litre)
ENGINE	Straight 6, 4235cc
HORSEPOWER	245bhp @ 5500rpm
TRANSMISSION	Automatic 3-speed
CHASSIS	Unitary construction
SUSPENSION	Independent front and rear
BRAKES	Girling disc
TOP SPEED	193km/h (120mph)
ACCELERATION	0-96km/h (60mph): 10.1 seconds

quietness and general good manners which many commentators judged to be superior to those of Rolls-Royce.

The XJ6 was updated in Series II form for the 1974 season. Identifiable by a squatter radiator grille and higher bumper line, the 2.8 version was phased out in 1973 to be later replaced in 1975 by the more familiar 3.4 litre unit. Mention should also be made of a handsome pillarless 4.2 litre coupé version of the design. Just 6505 examples were built between 1975 and 1977.

Sadly by this time an otherwise superlative product was beginning to suffer from poor build quality, a problem that, alas, infected the Series III version of 1979.

Sir William Lyons had retired in 1972, so with Jaguar having lost its stylistic mainspring, the Series III updating was undertaken with great sensitivity and competence by the Italian styling house of Pininfarina. The result was the definitive XJ6 with the window area increased and lines subtly redefined.

The long haul back began in 1980 with John Egan's arrival at Browns Lane. Quality improved and by the time that the XJ6 ceased production in 1986 its reputation had returned to levels that had greeted its announcement 18 years before.

Jaguar E-Type Series III

THE E-Type was the first recipient of Jaguar's long-awaited V12 engine that made its corporate debut in the Series III model of 1971.

As already recounted, the company had been toying with a V12 engine for its sports racers since the 1950s. Eventually destined for the XJ6 saloon, the 5.3 litre unit used single overhead camshafts per cylinder bank rather than the more complex and expensive competition-related twins.

Unlike its six-cylinder predecessors, the Series III was made with a common wheelbase, inherited from the two-plus-two coupé. It could be outwardly identified by its larger radiator air intake, complete with chromium plated grille, and disc, as opposed to wire, wheels. These were wider than their predecessors and required flared arches to accommodate them.

The roadster and coupé options were

perpetuated and the use of the longer wheelbase meant that the closed version perpetuated the provision of rear seats.

The extra length also meant that, for the first time, it was possible to produce an E-Type roadster with automatic transmission, the option having hitherto been restricted to the two-plus-two coupé.

A further refinement was provided by power assisted steering and, in truth, the Series III E-Type was more of a grand tourer than out and out sports car.

However, its top speed of 235km/h (146mph) was on a par with the original 3.8 but the emphasis

Jaguar's long-awaited V12 engine made its appearance in the Series III E-Type in 1971. Both cars date from 1972.

SPECIFICATION	JAGUAR E-TYPE SERIES III
ENGINE	V12, 5343cc
HORSEPOWER	272bhp @ 5850rpm
TRANSMISSION	Manual 4-speed
CHASSIS	Monocoque cockpit
SUSPENSION	Independent front and rear
BRAKES	Hydraulic disc
TOP SPEED	235km/h (146mph)
ACCELERATION	0-96km/h (60mph): 8.9 seconds

was on smoothness and the turbine-like efficiency provided by the 12-cylinder engine.

Sadly for the Series III, its production coincided with the petrol price rise of 1973 which damaged sales of what was by then an ageing model, both in Britain and on the all important American market.

The coupé ceased production that year, although the roadster survived until 1974. Those open cars destined for the US had also been disfigured by the presence of ungainly rubber bumper overriders, as required by increasingly stringent safety regulations.

News of the E-Type's demise was broken early in 1975. The production total of 14,983 V12s was split almost evenly between open and closed cars. The last 50 right-hand-drive roadsters were finished in black and carried a dashboard plaque signed by Sir William Lyons, by then in retirement.

So after 14 years Jaguar's last and most famous sports car bowed out and with it went a line that reached back to the S.S.90 of 1935.

There have been further performance models since then, but none possessed the lines, allure and sheer magic that ensured the letter E became the most sacred in the Jaguar lexicon.

Jaguar XJ12

JAGUAR'S long anticipated V12 engine, having first appeared in the 1971 E-Type, found its true destination the following year in the acclaimed XJ6 saloon.

Here was a model that transported its occupants at speeds of over 217km/h (135mph) in only the way that a 5.3 litre 12-cylinder engine could, even if fuel consumption was in the region of 23 litres/100km (12mpg). Three-speed automatic transmission was fitted as standard. The long wheelbase XJ12L followed in 1972.

The XJ range was uprated in Series II form in 1973 and, in 1975, the V12's four Zenith carburettors were replaced by a more efficient fuel injection system.

Sadly, the Series III generation of XJs coincided with soaring petrol prices, triggered by the 1973 Arab/Israeli war, and it was perhaps for this reason that, with the arrival of the injection engine, the model's name was changed from XJ12 to XJ5.3. Later, in 1977, the car was fitted with an improved GM400 automatic transmission but fuel consumption still lingered around the 21 litres/100km (13mpg) mark.

Like the six-cylinder Series II model, there was also a coupé version of the V12 family, produced in limited numbers between 1975 and 1977.

In 1979 came the Pininfarina-refined Series III XJ Series but once again a second fuel-crisis-induced recession was an unfavourable climate for a V12-engined model.

SPECIFICATION	JAGUAR XJ12
ENGINE	V12, 5343cc
HORSEPOWER	250bhp @ 6000rpm
TRANSMISSION	Automatic 3-speed
CHASSIS	Unitary construction
SUSPENSION	Independent front and rear
BRAKES	Girling disc
TOP SPEED	222km/h (138mph)
ACCELERATION	0-96km/h (60mph): 7.4 seconds

Later, in 1981, a much needed HE, for High Efficiency, 299bhp engine arrived, which saw an improvement in fuel consumption to 17 litres/100km (16mpg).

Right: The Series III XJ12 was introduced in 1979.
Below: It was only available with automatic transmission.

Although the six-cylinder XJs were replaced by a new car in 1986, the 12-cylinder Series III continued in production. This was because the Browns Lane engineers feared that they might be forced by Jaguar's Leyland parent to use the in-house Rover V8 engine. So they ensured that its replacement was structurally unable, without major modification, to accept a V configuration unit!

So the 1979-styled car remained in production until 1993, during which time it was rechristened, in 1983, the Sovereign V12, in place of the XJ name, but the familiar initials were restored in 1989.

Inevitably these Series III cars were the most numerous members of the family, making this Jaguar by far and away the world's most successful V12-powered saloon.

Jaguar XJS

A REPLACEMENT for the E-Type but not its successor, the XJS coupé has developed into a remarkably enduring and distinctive grand tourer.

It was not, initially, the happiest of Jaguar models. Essentially styled by Malcolm Sayer, its lines in general and the distinctive rear 'flying buttresses' in particular, were perhaps the least satisfactory feature of the design. The interior also lacked the traditional luxury of the Jaguar saloons.

The 241km/h (150mph) car was launched in 1975 in the middle of the energy crisis. Then just as the XJ-S (it was to lose its hyphen in 1991) seemed to be becoming established, along came an even more damaging petrol price hike. Little wonder that the car virtually ceased production in 1980/81 .

Although a manual version was listed, the majority of XJ-Ss were automatic cars and a much needed and more economical HE (high efficiency) version appeared in 1981. It was also the beneficiary of a greatly improved interior with wood veneer and leather replacing an apparent excess of plastic and vinyl.

There were further petrol-saving initiatives in the pipeline and, in 1983, the XJ-S became the first Jaguar to be fitted with the new 3.6 litre AJ6, twin-overhead-camshaft, six-cylinder, aluminium engine which was being developed for the as yet unannounced XJ6 saloon. Inevitably slower than its V12-powered stablemate, nevertheless the six was a 220km/h (137mph) car.

There had been no open Jaguar since the Series III E-Type was discontinued in 1975 and, with the arrival of the smaller engine in 1983, came a cabriolet version of the six.

This had a detachable Targa-type roof panel in the manner of the Porsche 911, and was built for Jaguar by Aston Martin Tickford until the factory took over in 1985. The concept was then extended to the 12-cylinder engine and the cabriolet was produced until 1987.

The XJS was available in convertible two-seater form from 1988 and was consequently bereft of the model's controversial 'flying buttresses'.

In 1988 came a true convertible version which was visually less cluttered than its predecessor and fitted with an electrically operated hood. This required more modifications than might have been outwardly apparent and necessitated a new front sub-frame to reduce scuttle shake. It was only built in V12 form.

The XJS benefited from across-the-range increases in engine capacity; in 1991 the six was enlarged to 4 litres and the following year an open version appeared, whilst the V12 went to 6 litres in 1993.

Both cars were produced until April 1996. They have been replaced by the new XK8 models which, like the XJS, are to be built in open and closed forms.

SPECIFICATION	JAGUAR XJS (V12)
ENGINE	V12, 5343cc
HORSEPOWER	285bhp @ 5750rpm
TRANSMISSION	Automatic 3-speed
CHASSIS	Unitary construction
SUSPENSION	Independent front and rear
BRAKES	Girling disc
TOP SPEED	246km/h (153mph)
ACCELERATION	0-96km/h (60mph): 6.7 seconds

Right: The Jaguar XJS in its original coupé guise.

61

Below: The XJS convertible acquired additional rear seats in 1992.

Jaguar XJ6

THE 18-year-old XJ6 was replaced by a new saloon of the same name in 1986. Visually related to its distinguished predecessor, it benefited from better aerodynamics and was significantly lighter. The low volume XJ12 excepted, the new XJ6 was the first Jaguar saloon since 1950 not to be powered by the legendary XK engine which effectively ceased production.

Developed under the XJ40 coding, it was powered by the more economical alloy AJ6 twin-cam six that had already appeared in the XJ-S of three years before.

Available in more refined twin-overhead-camshaft, 24 valve, 3.6 litre form, there was a new supplementary single-cam, 2.9 litre version with two, as opposed to four, valves per cylinder that had

SPECIFICATION	JAGUAR XJ6 (3.6 litre)
ENGINE	Straight 6, 3590cc
HORSEPOWER	221bhp @ 5000rpm
TRANSMISSION	Manual 5-speed
CHASSIS	Unitary construction
SUSPENSION	Independent front and rear
BRAKES	Girling disc
TOP SPEED	219km/h (136mph)
ACCELERATION	0-96km/h (60mph): 7.4 seconds

The new generation XJ6 was built between 1986 and 1994.

evolved from a single V12 cylinder bank. Both sixes were offered with a choice of a five-speed manual gearbox or an automatic one.

Mechanically the new car followed the layout of its famous forebear with all-round independent suspension which was uprated and lightened. Disc brakes were once again fitted all round but the rears were now located outboard, rather than inboard where they had resided since 1961.

Following the discontinuance of the Daimler Sovereign version of the XJ6 in 1983, the name became a Jaguar one. It had been applied to the more luxurious version of the model. This option was

perpetuated on the new six and it benefited from anti-lock brakes, cruise control and air conditioning.

Top speed for the 3.6 was in excess of 217km/h (135mph); that was also significantly quicker than the 4.2 litre Series III which was capable of 201km/h (125mph). Acceleration was accordingly better whilst handling and ride were also improved.

In 1989 engine capacity was increased with the 3.6 twin cam being enlarged to 4 litres. The 2.9 followed suit in 1990 with a rise to 3.2 litres and the replacement of the single camshaft with twins, so bringing it into line with the larger capacity six.

This two-engine range was perpetuated until

1993 when they were joined by a 12-cylinder version. The Series III 5.3 litre XJ12 had ceased production in 1992, but the new model had a more powerful, torquier 6 litre engine. The net result was a faster car, capable of 249km/h (155mph), rather than 222km/h (138mph). It was distinguished from the sixes by a gold radiator grille and alloy wheels. Although produced as a Jaguar, it was also built under the Daimler Double Six name.

Yet despite the undoubted improvements so apparent in this second generation XJ6, it did perhaps lack the flair and individuality of the Series III car. It continued in this form until 1994.

Jaguar XJR-9

IN 1988 Jaguar once again won the Le Mans 24 hour race after an interval of 31 years. It was a statement to the world that, after a traumatic decade, the company was once again a force to be reckoned with on both road and track.

But, as will become apparent, the racing route was a convoluted one and it began, not in industrially fraught Britain of the 1970s, but in Jaguar's mainstream market of America. It was there, in 1974, that at the nadir of the fuel crisis too many V12 E-Types were remaining unsold in dealers' showrooms.

President of British Leyland Motors Inc., Graham Whitehead, and vice president Mike Dale succeeded in cajoling Jaguar's corporate parent in London into supporting an E-Type racing program with the intention of kick-starting trans-Atlantic sales.

On the east coast the competition initiative was placed in the capable hands of Bob Tullius' Group 44 organization whilst Joe Huffaker was responsible for the western one.

The programme began in 1974 and, in the following year, Tullius succeeded in winning the Sports Car Club of America National B Championship for Jaguar.

Group 44 continued to campaign the E-Type's XJ-S V12-engined replacement and this in turn led to the arrival in 1982 of a completely new car.

It differed radically from its predecessors in not being based on a production model. It had a purpose-designed new chassis, the 575bhp V12-powered XJR-5 having been developed by Lee Dykstra's Special Chassis Inc., of Grand Rapids, Michigan.

A Group 44 racing programme got underway in the States and represented Jaguar, although without success, in Europe by returning to Le Mans in 1984 and again in 1985. But by this time the company had decided to back the rival UK-based,

SPECIFICATION	JAGUAR XJR-9
ENGINE	V12, 7 litres
HORSEPOWER	720bhp @ 7250rpm
TRANSMISSION	Manual 5-speed
CHASSIS	Carbon fibre composites monocoque
SUSPENSION	Independent front and rear
BRAKES	Automotive Products disc
TOP SPEED	386km/h (240mph)
ACCELERATION	N/A

Tony Southgate-designed, similarly configured 6 litre XJR-6, built for Group C competition by Tom Walkinshaw Racing of Kidlington, Oxfordshire.

Completed in 1985, teams ran at Le Mans in 1986 and 1987 with the XJR-8 although in both instances the Jaguars proved to be no match for the Porsche opposition. However, in 1987, the XJR-8 gave Jaguar its first-ever world sportscar championship victory.

Left: Line-up of XJR-9s at Le Mans in 1988. Below: Tom Walkinshaw's XJR-12-based XJR-15 road car of 1990 could also be used on the track.

Daly/Cogan/Perkins XJR-9 was 4th at Le Mans in 1988.

Then, in 1988, no less than five XJR-9s were entered for Le Mans; one was victorious and another came in fourth place. It was the first Jaguar triumph at the Sarthe circuit since 1957 and an emotional moment for chairman Sir John Egan (knighted in 1986).

A further victory followed in 1990 with XJR-12s in first and second places, to bring to seven Jaguar's triumphs in the 24 hour classic race. There could be little doubt that the big cat was back!

Jaguar XJR-S and XJR

THE XJR-S coupé was the first product of JaguarSport, a joint business set up by the company and Tom Walkinshaw's racing group. Initially modifications were confined to handling but later more power produced a faster yet still comfortable car.

In May 1988 came news of JaguarSport's formation, a £5 million venture created with the aim of producing around 500 cars a year from Walkinshaw's Kidlington premises. Cars would be based on production Jaguars and incorporate body and mechanical modifications to enhance their performances.

SPECIFICATION	JAGUAR XJR-S (6 litre)
ENGINE	V12, 5993cc
HORSEPOWER	318bhp @ 3750rpm
TRANSMISSION	Automatic 3-speed
CHASSIS	Unitary construction
SUSPENSION	Independent front and rear
BRAKES	Teves anti-lock disc
TOP SPEED	241km/h (150mph)
ACCELERATION	0-96km/h (60mph): 7.1 seconds

Below: A black radiator grille, front spoiler and sill moulding identifies JaguarSports' XJR saloon, built 1988-1992.

The first of these, the XJR-S, announced three months later, was outwardly identifiable by its body colour bumpers, sill extensions, rear spoiler and new wheels and tyres. Mechanical changes were confined to stiffer suspension and heavier steering although the 5.3 litre, 290bhp V12 engine and automatic transmission remained unchanged.

A year later, in 1989, the XJR-S became the first recipient of an enlarged 6 litre V12 with 318bhp on tap. Whilst the top speed of over 241km/h (150mph) was not much more than the mainstream XJS, it was torquier and more accelerative. There were more changes in the pipeline.

In 1991 more power came in the form of the V12 boosted to 333bhp, a claimed top speed of 254km/h (158mph) with 96km/h (60mph) coming up in just 5.8 seconds.

The XJR-S thus secured a useful niche in the Jaguar model line for the owner who wanted to combine the comfort of a grand tourer with the acceleration of a true sports cars.

The XJR was JaguarSport's version of the XJ saloon line – the approach followed that of the XJR-S – with modifications initially made to the car's handling and interior. Engine improvements followed later.

When announced in August 1988 the XJR was based on the 3.6 litre version of the XJ6 and was only available with four-speed automatic transmission.

The model differed visually from the standard car with the fitment of a black radiator grille, and colour-keyed bumper, wing mirrors and rear spoiler.

As there were no changes made to the engine, a top speed of 230km/h (143mph) was essentially the same as the Browns Lane-built model.

In 1989 the twin-cam six was enlarged to 4 litres on the mainstream XJ6 and top-end breathing was improved with an increase in power from 235bhp to 251bhp on the XJR.

In June 1990 came further revisions to the model to coincide with the arrival of an export version aimed at Europe in general and Germany in particular.

Above: The 1988 XJR-S Celebration coupé, number 54 of 100, created to celebrate Jaguar's Le Mans victory that year. Right: The interior of this model featured a leather-bound steering wheel and matching gear lever knob.

But whilst demand for the saloon's XJR-S stablemate remained steady, the XJR generated less interest and ceased production in 1992.

Jaguar XJ220 Show Car

JAGUAR'S sensational XJ220 supercar evolved from a similarly named coupé that was created to appear at the 1988 British Motor Show where it was greeted with universal acclaim.

In December 1984 Jaguar's engineering supremo, Jim Randle, drew up the specifications for a 500bhp car very much in the spirit of Ferrari's potent F40 and Porsche's costly and exclusive four-wheel-drive 959. As top speed was anticipated as being well in excess of 322 km/h (200mph), it was allotted the XJ220 name.

Randle was given the green light by chairman John Egan to proceed with the project, provided that work on the vehicle was undertaken after hours and at weekends. Participating members of the engineering team, therefore, became recruits of the exclusive 'Saturday Club'. What was a very cost-conscious exercise was helped by the support of many of Jaguar's suppliers.

The single car was completed just in time to appear at the 1988 Show, held at Birmingham's National Exhibition Centre, where it proved to be a major attraction.

Jaguar's magnificent V12 engine appeared in a unique 6.2 litre 500bhp form and with 48 valve twin-overhead-camshaft cylinder heads, as opposed to the customary single cams. It was mounted amidships and the use of an FF Developments' transmission system meant that all the 220's wheels were driven ones. Adaptive suspension was employed and anti-lock brakes completed the car's sophisticated mechanicals.

In view of the engine's location, this was a true two-seater and the sensational coupé body, styled by Keith Helfet, was dominated by elongated side-located air intakes for the mid-positioned V12. A further notable feature was the vertically actuated scissor-type doors.

The 220's appearance showed that the recently privatized Jaguar Cars clearly meant business and, in view of the rapturous reception that greeted the car, there was talk of putting it into production.

After the closure of the event, it was evaluated by the newly established JaguarSport, set up collaboratively by the company and racing car constructor Tom Walkinshaw. Not until December 1989, after Ford had taken control of Jaguar, did the company decide to proceed with the project.

Unlike the original car, the 220 would not be built at Browns Lane but at a new manufacturing facility established by Walkinshaw at Bloxham, Oxfordshire. It would be a further three and half years before deliveries actually began.

Left: The XJ220 was an uncompromising two-seater with a luxurious interior. Below and opposite: The fabulous lines of the 1988 mid-V12-engined, four-wheel-drive show car. The rear spoiler was electrically adjustable.

SPECIFICATION	JAGUAR XJ 220
ENGINE	V12, 6222cc
HORSEPOWER	Over 500bhp @ 7000rpm
TRANSMISSION	Manual, 5-speed
CHASSIS	Riveted and bonded alloy sheet
SUSPENSION	Independent front and rear
BRAKES	Automotive Products disc
TOP SPEED	Over 322km/h (200mph)
ACCELERATION	N/A

69

Right: Jaguar's Keith Helfet was responsible for the 220's magnificent styling. Below: The scissors doors did not reach the production version. Bottom: All-important cooling ducts for the mighty V12 became a significant stylistic feature.

Jaguar XJ220

THE 220 entered production in 1992, by which time Europe and America were in the grip of an economic recession that adversely affected its sales potential. But this did not detract from the fact that the sleek coupé was one of the world's fastest cars with a claimed top speed of 343km/h (213mph).

When news broke at the end of 1989 that the 220 was to enter production, it was priced at £361,000, index-linked to the delivery date, with customers required to place a £50,000 deposit. A minimum of 220 cars would be built and total production not breach the 350 mark.

The 220 was duly launched in October 1991 at the Tokyo Motor Show and although outwardly similar to the 1988 car, beneath the surface it had been radically re-engineered. Whilst the overall length remained at 4879mm (16ft), the wheelbase, at 2640mm (8ft 8in), was about 203mm (8in) less.

This reflected the fitment of a new engine because the mighty V12 had been replaced by the visually less impressive but nonetheless immensely powerful 3.5 litre, twin-turbocharged V6, as used in the XJR-11 sports racer. It developed an astounding 542bhp which compared with some 500 for the V12.

Whilst the 1988 prototype had employed four-wheel drive, the production 220 was a rear-drive machine and the anti-lock brakes, adaptive suspension and scissor doors had succumbed to the realities of the production line.

But the 220 was one of the world's truly great supercars with stunning looks, performance and formidable roadholding whilst also being sufficiently civilized for everyday motoring. Top speed was in excess of 337km/h (210mph).

These figures were bettered by the arrival in 1993 of a lightened racing version, the 220-C, and a trio of these cars ran at that year's Le Mans event.

Less desirably, another accelerating graph was that of the car's price. By the time of the 220's October 1991 launch, this had risen to £403,000 and a number of customers who had already

The first example of the V6-engined XJ220 production car in 1992.

pledged deposits found, in a changed economic world, that they were unable to take delivery.

Yet a further complication was the appearance, in 1990, of Walkinshaw's faster, more expensive and exclusive V12-engined XJR-15, based on the Le Mans winning XJR-12.

A protracted legal dialogue then ensued and, in September 1993, Jaguar announced that those customers who wished to buy themselves out of their contracts could do so. By the time that the last 220 was built in 1994, a total of 275 examples of this delectable Jaguar had been completed.

The XJ220's wheelbase was shorter than the show car's.

SPECIFICATION	JAGUAR XJ220
ENGINE	V6, 3498cc
HORSEPOWER	542bhp @ 7000rpm
TRANSMISSION	Manual, 5-speed
CHASSIS	Riveted and bonded alloy sheet
SUSPENSION	Independent front and rear
BRAKES	Ventilated disc
TOP SPEED	In excess of 338km/h (210mph)
ACCELERATION	0-100km/h (62mph): 4 seconds

Jaguar XJ6

JAGUAR'S current mainstream model, the XJ6 saloon, was impressively revised in 1994 with the result that it is faster, quieter and better built than its predecessor. Thus reinvigorated it is destined to remain in production until 1998.

Ford, Jaguar's owner since 1989, has spent £200 million on what was coded project X300, of which some £110 million was allocated to the manufacturing process.

The most obvious difference between the revised XJ6 and earlier versions is a new headlamp layout with the recessed quadruple lamps replaced by a more bulbous presentation. The tail has also been outwardly and inwardly redesigned so that the boot can now accommodate two sets of golf clubs!

Under the bonnet the redesignated AJ16 alloy, six-cylinder, twin-overhead-camshaft engine had been a beneficiary of more than 100 newly tooled parts. The result is a more powerful and smoother running unit that also offers better fuel economy than its AJ6 predecessor.

The model is available in two sizes, of 3.2 and 4 litres, with a manual five-speed Getrag gearbox or an automatic ZF unit which is standardized on the V12 and a new XJR version.

The smaller 200bhp 3.2 six has been a noteworthy beneficiary of the engine redesign and, say Jaguar, is capable of 223km/h (139mph).

In its 4 litre form the XJ6 is a 231km/h (144mph) car, while the XJR is the top-line supercharged model with the power boosted from 246bhp in the mainstream saloon to 321bhp.

Outwardly identifiable by its wire mesh radiator grille in place of the usual slatted one, it is also shod with larger 431mm (17in) alloy wheels. All this combines to produce a 246km/h (153mph) car with sparkling acceleration to match.

Left: The XJ Executive version with optional alloy wheels.

SPECIFICATION	JAGUAR XJ6 (4 litres auto)
ENGINE	Straight 6, 3980cc
HORSEPOWER	246bhp @ 4800rpm
TRANSMISSION	Automatic 4-speed
CHASSIS	Unitary construction
SUSPENSION	Independent front and rear
BRAKES	ITT Automotive anti-lock disc
TOP SPEED	231km/h (144mph)
ACCELERATION	0-96km/h (60mph): 7.8 seconds

Whilst the six-cylinder engines have benefited from extensive revision, Jaguar's long-running V12 has been carried over without modification from the previous series. This is because the 6 litre unit is destined to cease production at the end of 1996, when it will be replaced by a new V8.

But it still provides 241km/h (150mph) plus motoring with all the smoothness and refinement associated with the configuration. Available in Jaguar XJ12 and Daimler Double Six guises, they will mark the end of an engine line that first appeared back in 1971.

Top: The potent top line XJR version, with identifying wire mesh grille, powered by a supercharged, 4 litre, six-cylinder engine. Above: The automatic XJ Executive's cockpit.

Jaguar XK8

THE 35th anniversary of the launch of the E-Type at the Geneva Motor Show was marked at the 1996 event by the surprise appearance of the XK8 coupé.

A convertible version was appropriately announced at the New York event in April, which was the location of the debut of the E-Type roadster in 1961. Both versions went on sale in October 1996 when they replaced the 21-year-old XJS.

In fact the E, discontinued in 1975, was to have been succeeded by what was popularly dubbed the F-Type sports car but this was sidelined by Ford soon after it took control of Jaguar in 1989. It did, however, represent the starting point of Ford-owned Aston Martin's DB7 of 1993.

Like that model, the XK8 uses as its basis the XJS platform, whilst its name is intended to evoke memories, particularly on the all important American market, of the XK 120/150 family and the E-Type which was known in the 'States as the XKE.

The 8 in the title refers to a new 4 litre, all alloy V8 engine with twin overhead camshafts per cylinder bank, which is Jaguar's first, and is to be built by Ford at its plant at Bridgend in South Wales. It is expected to endow the new model with a top speed exceeding the 241km/h (150mph) mark.

Initially there will be no manual gearbox versions available so, for the first two years or so, all XK8s will be fitted with a five-speed ZF automatic unit.

Responsibility for the car's external styling is vested in Geoff Lawson, who joined Jaguar as chief stylist in 1984. Whilst there is some family resemblance to the E-Type and XJ13 prototype, the two-plus-two XK8 is not aimed at the relatively limited sports car market but at the more lucrative one dominated by the Mercedes-Benz SL.

The XK8 has enjoyed a four-year gestation. Work on the project, coded X100, began in January 1992 and both versions of the model received the corporate green light in October, just 10 months later. With 12,000 examples of the XK8 destined to be produced in 1997, some 40 per cent will be convertibles. As in the past, about 20 per cent of the output will remain in the UK with the balance crossing the Atlantic. There it is anticipated that the open car will account for an overwhelming majority of sales.

Despite the XK8's very different target market, there have been the inevitable comparisons with the E-Type, although it remains to be seen whether this latest Jaguar will be accorded the acclaim of its legendary predecessor.

Far left: Jaguar's first V8, and only the fourth new engine in its history, the alloy AJ26 will power the XK8. A 4 litre 32-valve unit with twin overhead camshafts per cylinder bank, it will also eventually replace the XJ6's straight six engine. It is shorter, lighter, more economical and powerful than its predecessor. Left: The XK8 cockpit which perpetuates Jaguar's well-proven walnut and leather combination. The car will initially only be available with automatic transmission. Below: The convertible version of the XK8 which has a double-lined, electrically operated hood.

SPECIFICATION	JAGUAR XK8
ENGINE	V8, 3996cc
HORSEPOWER	290bhp @ 6100rpm
TRANSMISSION	Automatic 5-speed
CHASSIS	Unitary construction
SUSPENSION	Independent front and rear
BRAKES	Hydraulic disc
TOP SPEED	241km/h (155mph)
ACCELERATION	0-96km/h (60mph): 6.6 seconds

Above: Aiming at an exclusive market, the XK8 coupé of 1996 with a distinguished predecessor, a 1970 Series II E-Type coupé, in the background.

Opposite above: A Jaguar coupé for the 21st century; it is expected that the majority of XK8s will be sold in America. Jaguar's Geoff Lawson styled both coupé and convertible.

Opposite below: The XK8 convertible. As with the coupé, the accent is very much on refinement. The convertible will account for some 40 per cent of total production.

Index

Page numbers in **bold** type refer to illustrations.